LEAPFROGGING THROUGH WETLANDS

By
Margaret Anderson
Nancy Field
Karen Stephenson

Illustrated by Michael Maydak

Computer Designer Betsy True

Text copyright © 1998 Dog-Eared Publications
Text copyright © 2005 Margaret Anderson, Karen Stephenson and Nancy Field
Artwork copyright © 1998 Michael Maydak

Third Printing 2006

ISBN-10: 0-941042-18-9

ISBN-13: 978-0-941042-18-5

 Printed in the USA

Leapfrogging through Wetlands

Ribbit! Ribbit! Ribbit!

Spring is in the air. The marsh is alive with the sound of music — frog music! Only the male frogs take part in the chorus. They are calling the females back to the water. It's time to lay eggs to start the next generation.

Frogs are **amphibians**. The word "amphibian" means "double life." Amphibians are animals that live both on land and in water. Most frogs spend their young stages in water and their adult life on land. When the tadpoles first hatch from the eggs, they are more like fish than frogs. They have no legs and swim around with finlike tails. They breathe through gills. As they get bigger, they lose their tails, grow legs and develop lungs. They are ready to leave the water.

Wetlands also lead a double life. They, too, belong both to the water and to the land. Sometimes wetlands are more water than land. Sometimes they are more land than water.

As you go leapfrogging through this book, you'll learn why wetlands are important. They are giant cafeterias that offer a huge variety of food. They provide nursery space for the young stages of many **species** (kinds) of birds, frogs, and other animals. They are wild places where even some of the plants eat animals!

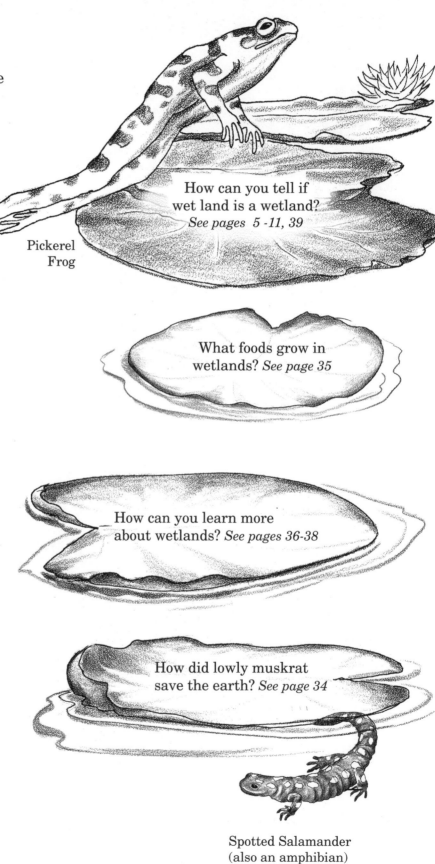

Pickerel Frog

How can you tell if wet land is a wetland? *See pages 5 -11, 39*

What foods grow in wetlands? *See page 35*

How can you learn more about wetlands? *See pages 36-38*

How did lowly muskrat save the earth? *See page 34*

Spotted Salamander (also an amphibian)

What three clues are
used to identify a wetland?
See page 5

How do wetlands help us?
See pages 12-13, 35

Coot

Is the water in
wetlands ever salty?
See pages 16-19, 32-33

A Frog's Life Cycle

Tadpoles **Eggs**

**Older
Tadpoles**

Adult

Where do dragonflies live?
See pages 4, 15

What dangers do
migrating birds face?
Play the game on pages 25-27

Which animal is a
wetland engineer?
See page 14

Where do you find
wetlands in North America?
See pages 16-17

What are some different
types of freshwater wetlands?
See pages 20-24, 28-31

3

A Jump Back in Time

Eryops lived before the dinosaurs. It was an 8-foot long amphibian that looked like a huge frog with a tail. We don't know if the males made frog music, but we do know that Eryops shared the world with insects. Giant dragonflies patrolled the skies. Some had wings that measured 2 feet across.

Three hundred million years ago, North America was much wetter than it is now. The land was low and swampy. Strange plants grew in the swamps. When these plants died, they sank into the water and did not rot. Forests of new plants grew in their place. Slowly, the water level rose and drowned the forests. After millions of years, the drowned forests turned to coal. Those prehistoric wetland forests provide us with energy today. We call that long-ago time the Coal Age.

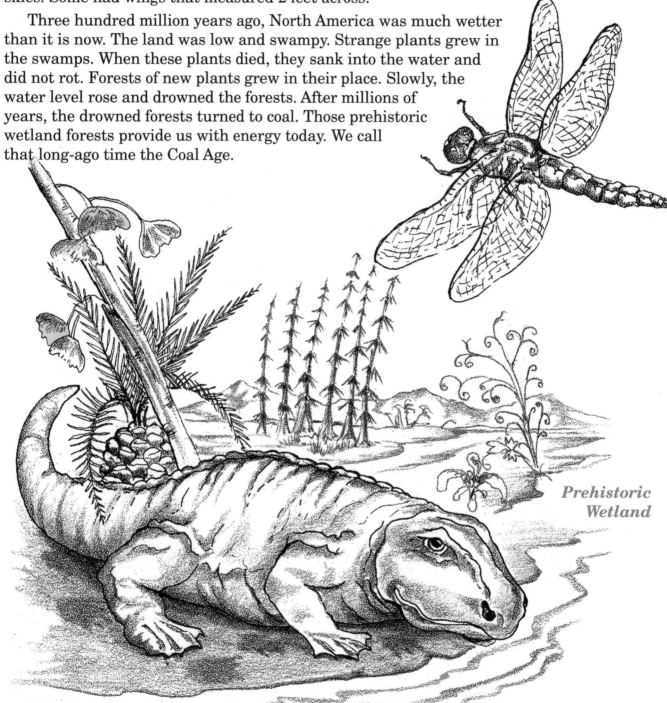

Prehistoric Wetland

Prehistoric wetlands were very different from our wetlands today. But even now, not all wetlands are alike. Wetlands near the coast, where the water is salty, are not like the freshwater wetlands in the bottomlands along rivers. Some wetlands are dry for part of the year. Some soggy areas are not wetlands. So how can we recognize a wetland? What do wetlands from different times and places have in common?

4

Wetland Detectives

Jim Boggs and Marsha Waters are wetland scientists. They are trying to sort out the true wetlands from the impostors. Luckily, they know the three clues to look for when trying to identify wet land (or even dry land) as a wetland.

Use these clues to complete the sentence at the bottom of the page. Then you, too, are ready to be a wetland detective.

Clue # 1:

It falls to the earth in the form of rain. The sun turns it to vapor to cycle again.

Clue # 2:

Farmers plow it, gardeners hoe, then plant their seeds all in row.

Clue # 3:

This kingdom has no king or queen. Its subjects are all dressed in green.

Freshwater Marsh

During at least part of the year wetlands are covered with (1) _____. This changes the (2)_____ and only certain types of (3)_____ are able to grow in it.

Answers on last page

Clue #1: The "Wet" in Wetlands

The first thing to look for when identifying a wetland is water. However, the amount of water in a wetland does not stay the same. Changes in the water level often go in cycles. In some cases, the cycle is regular and the time between cycles is short. In coastal wetlands, for example, the water level is tied to the rise and fall of the tides. In other places, changes happen over much longer time periods. In river bottomlands, the water is high during a flood. After the flood, water drains back into the river channel and the land dries out. In other wetlands, the water level rises during the rainy season. In dry weather, some of the water seeps into the ground to restore groundwater. Some water evaporates in the hot sun. Some is taken up by plants and escapes into the air.

Marsha Waters is trying to identify three tricky wetland suspects. The water level for each wetland keeps changing, but she's sure she can tell them apart. She says that knowing the pattern of the water level is as good as finding a clear set of fingerprints.

See if you can identify the wetlands on the next page from their wet-and-dry patterns. But first take a look at your own fingerprints.

Everybody's fingerprints are different, but they can be classified according to certain patterns. The most common patterns are arch, loop, and whorl. Which ones can you find in your fingerprint?

Arch

Loop

Whorl

Your fingerprint

Read these descriptions of three wetland suspects. Draw a line to the wetland "fingerprint" that matches it.

1

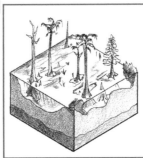

Florida cypress pond
A small, wet hollow where cypress trees are growing.
Hint: In Florida the wet season is in summer. Fall and spring tend to be dry.

A Morning Afternoon Evening Night

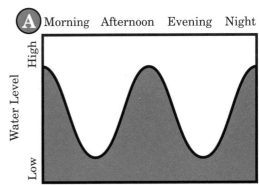

Water Level — High / Low

2

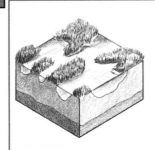

Coastal salt marsh
An area that is covered by sea water at high tide. The plants and animals have to adjust to being covered by water and then stranded on dry land twice each day.

B Spring Summer Fall Winter

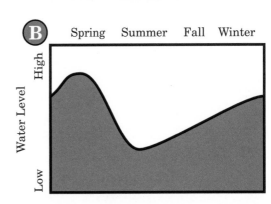

Water Level — High / Low

3

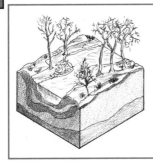

Bottomland floodplain
Lowlands found along streams and rivers. The floodplain is covered in water when the river overflows, especially as the snow melts in the spring.

C Spring Summer Fall Winter

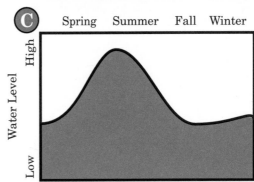

Water Level — High / Low

Answers on last page

This is a thumbprint frog. Make your own frog—sitting, leaping, and landing.

Clue #2: The "Land" in Wetlands

Now that Marsha has identified the wetlands by their fingerprints, she has taken on a new case. It is late summer and she is looking for a marsh that has cleverly disguised itself as a patch of dry land. With her face close to the ground, Marsha discovers her first clue — the soil.

What clue could there be in soil? It's just dirt, isn't it? Wrong! Soil is made up of bits of crushed rock, air, and water. It also contains dead plants and animals. Anything that was once living is called **organic matter**.

Marsha recognizes wetland soil by its color. She uses a book of color charts to help her. Soils that are flooded much of the time have very little oxygen and the plant material does not break down. These soils are black or very dark brown. Wetland soils with very little organic matter are called **mineral soils**. They are gray, green, or bluish gray. Marsha also looks for a reddish-brown "rusty" layer around the roots of plants that forms when oxygen in the roots acts on iron in the soil.

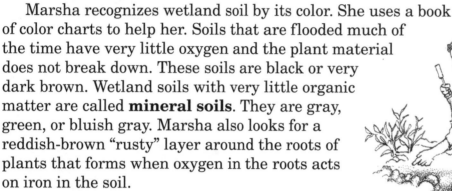

Color your own chart to help you catch wetland soil suspects. (These colors are found in a 64-color box of Crayola® Crayons.)

Wetland Suspect

☐ Black

☐ Gray

☐ Sea Green and Gray

☐ Brown and Gray

Probably Not Wetlands

☐ Goldenrod

☐ Bittersweet

☐ Tan

Wetland soil holds water like a sponge. It also acts as a filter. Here is how you can show it:

1 Cut away a a section from the top of each of three plastic bottles and punch holes in the bottom.

Some frogs spend the whole winter in mud at the bottom of a pond or marsh. They breathe through their skin.

2 Fill one with gravel, one with coarse sand, and one with soil (wetland soil, if you can get it.)

3 Now pour muddy water into each bottle and catch the drippings in a pan.

4 Which pan fills the fastest? Which pan has the cleanest water? Which is the best filter — gravel, sand, or soil?

Here are some words that Marsha often uses when she is talking about wetland soils. She calls them **hydric** soils. Hydric means wet. Because hydric soils contain no oxygen she says that they are **anaerobic**. Most bacteria that break down dead plants need oxygen. They cannot live in anaerobic soils, so plant material stays in the soil for a long time. It does not **decompose** (break down). However, some kinds of bacteria can live in anaerobic soils. They produce sulphur, the gas that gives rotten eggs a bad smell. That's why Marsha usually sniffs wetland soil. The rotten-egg smell is a give-away. Other kinds of bacteria produce a gas called methane or swamp gas. There's a lot of methane in cow manure, so you can guess what that smells like!

Answers on last page

Clue #3: The Plants in Wetlands

While Marsha was looking at the soil, Jim Boggs was thinking about plants. They have to do everything animals do — eat, breathe, avoid danger, and reproduce — while they are rooted in one spot. If a plant is hungry, it cannot chase down its food. If the air is bad, it cannot move to where the air is fresh. It can't run away from its enemies and it can't search for a mate. Nor can it move to higher ground during a flood, run from a fire, or find shelter during a freeze.

Draw your own cartoons to show how plants might act... if only they weren't stuck in one place:

Eating Out	Escaping

Dancing	Playing

Life is hard for a plant. It is even harder for a wetland plant. The soil is often poor quality and low in oxygen. The water level keeps changing. Wetland plants have developed special features to help them survive. These features are called **adaptations**. Hollow stems and air spaces inside roots are common adaptations in wetland plants.

Cattail

Bladderwort

Hollow stems and air spaces

Wetland plants can be divided into three groups.

Emergents stick up above the water surface. Cattails, arrowhead, sedges, and rushes are emergents. Cattail stems and leaves are like styrofoam® — full of air spaces, but lightweight and strong.

Floaters include rooted plants such as water lilies. The leaves have long flexible stems that adjust to changing water levels. Duckweed is a free floater that often forms a green carpet over ponds.

Submergents, such as coontail and bladderwort, live underwater. Bladderwort is unusual because it adds to its diet by eating animals. Tiny bladders on the leaves suck in water creatures as they pass by.

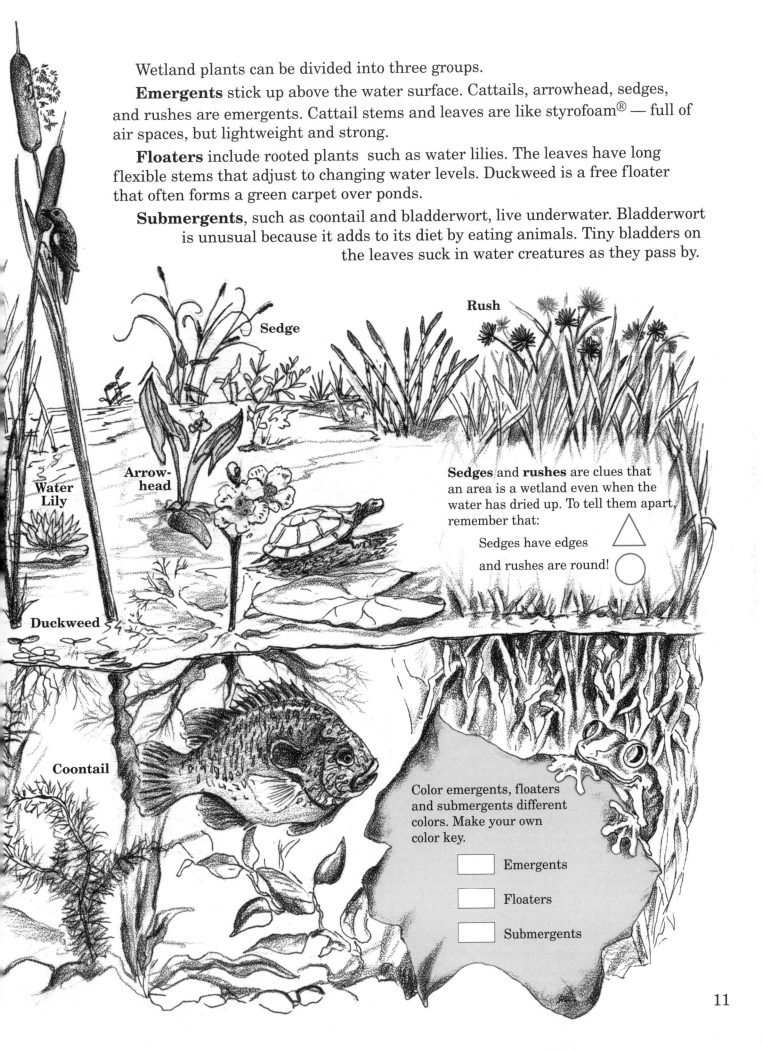

Rush

Sedge

Arrow-head

Water Lily

Duckweed

Coontail

Sedges and **rushes** are clues that an area is a wetland even when the water has dried up. To tell them apart, remember that:

Sedges have edges

and rushes are round!

Color emergents, floaters and submergents different colors. Make your own color key.

Emergents

Floaters

Submergents

How Wetlands Help Us

It isn't hard to think of three good reasons to preserve a forest. It isn't hard to think of three good reasons to preserve a lake. But most people find it harder to think of three good reasons to save a wetland. Swamps and bogs have an image problem. Even their names have a negative sound. We get swamped with homework and bogged down in math problems. It has taken us a long time to realize that we need wetlands.

Wetlands are, of course, important to the many kinds of animals and plants that live there. Young salmon live in river estuaries before going out to sea. Dragonflies grow up in swamp water. Birds nest in marshes and use them for rest stops during long flights. Turtles sun themselves on floating logs.

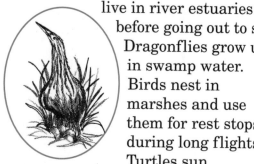

American bittern hiding among the grasses.

Wetlands are important to people, too. They provide a place to grow rice, cranberries, and blueberries. Most fish and shellfish spend some stage of their lives in wetlands. People visit wetlands to watch birds, canoe, hunt, fish, take pictures, and just to listen to the sounds and enjoy being outdoors.

Wetlands help us in other less obvious ways. They control flooding by soaking up some of the water like a sponge and then letting it seep out later on. They protect inland areas from strong winds and hurricanes. They clean the water by filtering out pollution. However, too much pollution can destroy a wetland.

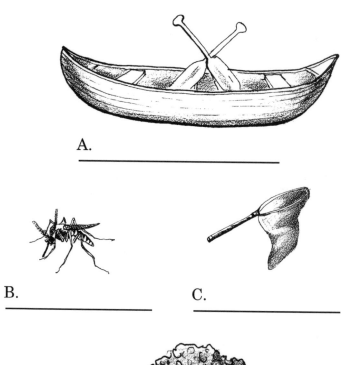

A.

_____

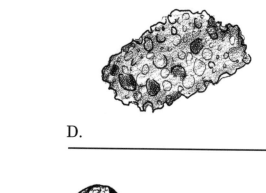

B.

_____

C.

_____

D.

_____

Pesky Mosquitoes

Most mosquito problems don't start in wetlands. Puddles, pop cans, buckets, and old tires, are attractive breeding sites.

Each of the pictures below stands for a wetland service. What service does each picture represent?

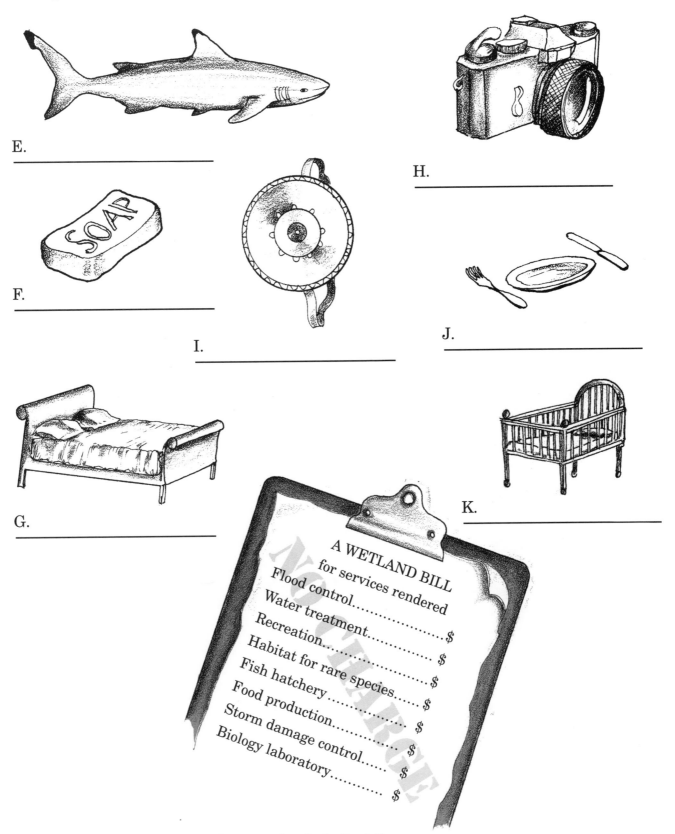

E. _____

F. _____

G. _____

H. _____

I. _____

J. _____

K. _____

A WETLAND BILL
for services rendered

Flood control........................ $

Water treatment............... $

Recreation...................... $

Habitat for rare species...... $

Fish hatchery.............. $

Food production............ $

Storm damage control...... $

Biology laboratory........... $

NO CHARGE

One of the great things about wetlands is that they perform their services for free, and they do many of them at the same time. Think what it would cost if a wetland sent a bill.

Answers on last page

Eager Beaver Engineers

Wetlands occur where water meets the land. Some formed when glaciers melted at the end of the last ice age. Some are found where rivers run into the sea. Some are on flood plains where rivers "store" water during floods.

People and wetlands often want the same land. We drain wetlands for building and farming. We use flat land for airports, soccer fields, and cities. We grow crops on flood plains. Once people realized how important wetlands are, laws were passed to protect them. If a wetland is destroyed, another has to be created somewhere else. This takes time and is not easy. Wetlands have their own types of soil and plants. We are not, however, alone in making new wetlands. Beaver engineers have been creating wetlands ever since the first beaver felled a tree.

The Eager Beavers have found a new place to live. They go to work felling trees. They dam the stream and build a house. Next they raise a family. Once the trees are gone, the beavers move on, and with no one to repair it, the dam breaks. Deer now browse the lush grass and shrubs that grow in the wet soil.

Arrange the pictures in the right order to tell how the beavers converted a forest to a wetland. _____

Answers on last page

Wetland Critters

The beaver pond and surrounding wetlands attract other animals, including insects. Many kinds of insect **larvae** (young stages) live in ponds. Baby mosquitoes turn somersaults and hang from the surface film. Caddisflies creep about in houses built from sticks or stones. Dragonfly larvae are the monsters of the deep, snapping at tadpoles. Young water beetles, called water tigers, can be recognized by their claw-like jaws. The adults live under water, too. You can tell mayfly and stonefly larvae apart by their tails. Mayflies have three tails and stoneflies have two.

Pair up these young water insects with the adults.

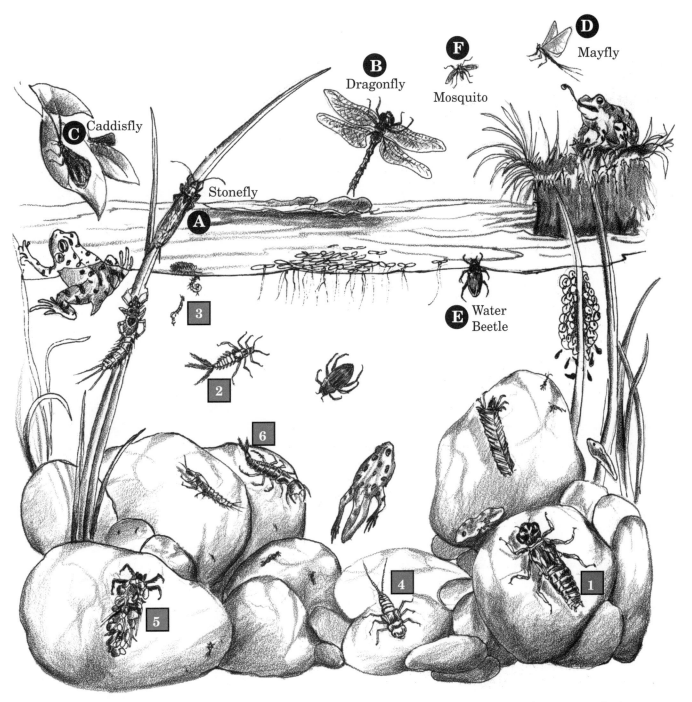

Look for the stages in a frog's life cycle.

Answers on last page

Wetland Hopping

Wetlands go by a lot of different names. Discover some of those names by traveling the wetland maze.

Visit each wetland without retracing your steps. Each site is marked by a symbol. Find the same symbol beside the maze and read about the main features of each wetland. Add a wetland in your area to the map. What are its main features?

 START

Saltwater Wetlands

 Saltwater Marsh
Tall grasses and other plants. Washed by salt tidewater twice a day.

 Mangrove Swamp
Mangrove trees grow on stilts. Tropical climate.

 Estuary
Partly enclosed body of water where salt water from the ocean and fresh water from rivers mix.

Label the marsh and the swamp.

A. _____

B. _____

Some names are reserved for wetlands in a particular region. Others describe the kind of wetland. A marsh, for example, is a grassy wetland, whereas a swamp has trees and shrubs. Some names have an interesting ring to them. Try saying these names out loud—muskeg, slough, bottomlands, bayou, quaking bog, and fen!

FINISH

Freshwater Wetlands

 Freshwater Marsh
Grasses, cattails, and other soft stemmed plants. Water from lakes, streams, melting snow, and rain.

 Shrub Swamp
Trees and woody shrubs. Often found near rivers and slow streams.

 Cypress Swamp
Cypress trees are the main plants.

 Prairie Pothole
Small marsh in places hollowed out long ago by melting glaciers.

 Bog
Mosses and acid-loving plants. Very poor drainage.

 Fen
Similar to bogs, but have moving water and are often less acidic.

 Playa
Temporary marshes found in southwestern deserts.

 Pocosin
Evergreen forested and scrub-shrub wetlands mainly in North Carolina.

Many kinds of wetlands — many kinds of frogs. There are nearly 4,000 different species of frogs and toads in the world.

Answers on last page

The Estuary Cafeteria

Osprey

An estuary forms where a river runs into the sea. The water in an estuary is less salty than ocean water, but more salty than river water. It is called **brackish** water. When a river reaches the sea, it usually slows down and fans out. The water loses its load of fine soil and mudflats build up. Mudflats are covered by salt water at high tide and are open to the air at low tide. They often smell like rotten eggs. Although a mudflat looks like a great wasteland, it is very rich in food. It gets its nutrients from both the river and from the sea.

In the estuary cafeteria, plants like eelgrass and seaweed provide places for dining and hiding. However, the diners can end up as someone else's dinner! **Phytoplankton** (tiny drifting plants) are eaten by **zooplankton** (tiny drifting animals). These are eaten by filter-feeders, such as clams, that are then eaten by shore birds. This chain of eat and be eaten is called a **food chain**. It all starts with energy from the sun.

Great Blue Heron

Snail

Young Salmon

Isopod

Crab

Zooplankton

Sun

Plant

Snail

Fish

Heron

Many animals eat more than one type of food. The food chains link up to form a food web. **Connect the animals to their food to make a food web.**

Answers on last page

18

Salt marshes are often found near estuaries. The plants and animals that live there have to cope with the tide covering the marsh with sea water twice a day. Salt grass gets rid off salt by collecting it in special glands. At low tide you can see the salt crystals shining on the leaves.

Why are there no frogs in this food web?

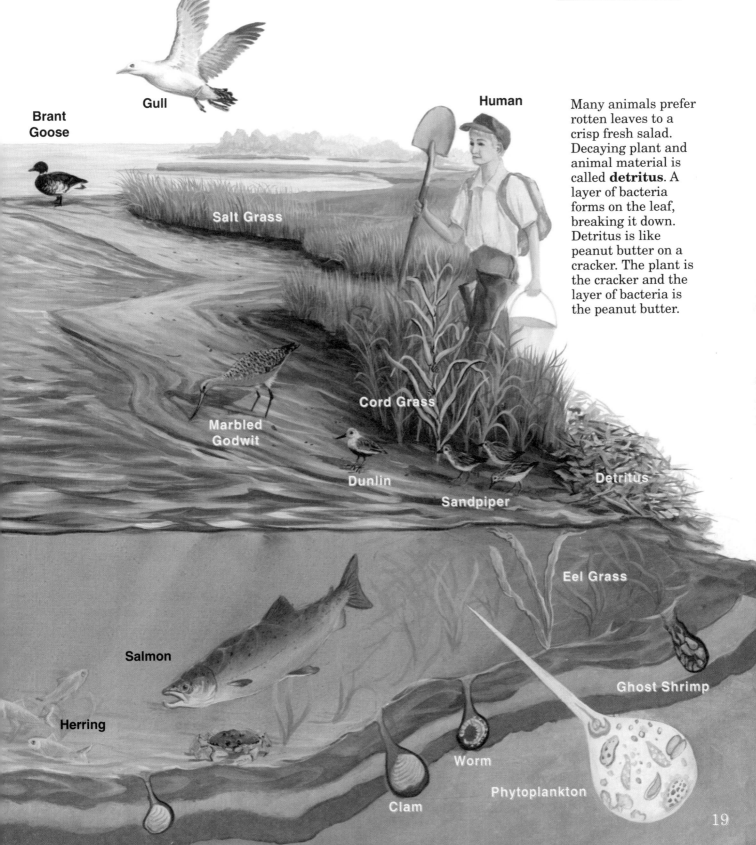

Gull

Brant Goose

Human

Salt Grass

Many animals prefer rotten leaves to a crisp fresh salad. Decaying plant and animal material is called **detritus**. A layer of bacteria forms on the leaf, breaking it down. Detritus is like peanut butter on a cracker. The plant is the cracker and the layer of bacteria is the peanut butter.

Marbled Godwit

Cord Grass

Dunlin

Sandpiper

Detritus

Eel Grass

Salmon

Ghost Shrimp

Herring

Worm

Clam

Phytoplankton

19

River of Grass

The Florida Everglades is a wide, slow, grassy river, draining out to the sea. It swarms with unusual wildlife. The anhinga swoops down after a fish. With a sideways swipe of its jaws an alligator snaps up the bird and then climbs onto the bank with a satisfied smile on its face. The alligator seems to be the "bad guy" of the swamp. You wouldn't ask one to babysit! You wouldn't want one for a landlord! Yet those are two of an alligator's important jobs.

In the dry season, alligators use their strong heads and bodies to dig out pools. These pools provide a home for fish and shrimp. Soon birds, turtles, and frogs move in. Other animals drop by looking for food and water. The alligator does not mind sharing his pond with so many tasty creatures!

Over time, canals, dikes, and dams have changed the flow of the water into the Everglades. Gator holes form important refuges. Without "alligator landlords" many kinds of animals and plants could not get through the dry season.

Alligators are reptiles, like lizards, snakes, and turtles, but in some ways they resemble birds. They make nests. They lay hard-shelled eggs and take care of their young.

The female builds a mound from mud and plants close to the water. She hollows out the top and lays about 40 eggs. After covering the eggs, she stays around and guards them from raccoons, opossums, and bears. Sometimes a turtle lays her eggs in the nest when the mother alligator isn't looking. Without knowing it, the alligator babysits the turtle eggs along with her own. Alligator nests are also good places for plants to take root and grow.

Can you think of three good things about an alligator?

Answer on last page

The Snail Kite Mystery

About 30 years ago, the snail kite population dropped to fifty birds. The species was **endangered**. It would soon be **extinct** — gone forever. What had gone wrong?

Biologists solved the mystery. The ponds where apple snails live were drying up and the snails were dying. The kite's curved beak is exactly right for picking apple snails out of their shells. Saving the birds meant first saving the snails. The biologists set about improving snail habitat. A series of wet years helped. The kite population gradually rose to 1000 birds.

Up to one third of all endangered species in North America live in or use wetlands sometime during their lives. Wetlands are endangered species havens.

21

At Home in the Shrub Swamp

Shrub swamps are often found around the edges of lakes and streams. In northern swamps, moose hide and give birth among alder and pussy willow shrubs. Deer and ruffed grouse eat the buds and twigs. Birds use the branches of willow and other shrubs for perching while looking for insects to eat. In the winter, willow branches stick up through the snow providing buds for ruffed grouse as well as twigs or bark for mammals. Forks in trees or shrubs provide protected nest sites. Willow leaves, sedges, horsetails and pond-weeds are favorite foods for several animals. Moist, mucky soil is home to worms — a tasty treat for some birds and animals. Starnose moles tunnel in the moist soil. Occasional visitors, like bears, feed on berries, skunk cabbage, horsetail plants, alder leaves and grubs. A bear can even eat a moose calf.

Study the picture of the northern shrub swamp.
Decide where you would find the following:
(More than one number can go in a blank.)

———— Water site for animals
———— Moose gives birth and hides her calf here
———— Moose food
———— Skunk cabbage grows here
———— Honey bees warm up here
———— Ruffed grouse food
———— Nest site for yellow warblers
———— Starnose moles tunnel here
———— Starnose mole food
———— Starnose mole nest site
———— Whitetailed deer food
———— Spiders wait here to ambush flies.
———— Alder flycatcher perch
———— Woodcock food
———— Striped Chorus Frog food
———— Bear food
———— Green heron hiding place

Answers on last page

Skunk cabbage starts growing early in the spring. Energy stored in its roots generates enough heat to melt leftover snow banks. The plant's warmth helps spread its "skunk-like" odor, which attracts pollinating insects. Inside the hood, or spathe, summer-like temperatures provide shelter for other insects.

All animals need food, water and shelter. They need somewhere to hide from enemies and somewhere to raise their young. The place where everything is arranged in a way that makes it possible for an animal or a plant to live is called its **habitat**.

23

Prairie Potholes–Duck Dive-ins

Ten thousand years ago, at the end of the last ice age, glaciers left holes in the northern plains. In the spring, these holes fill up with rain and run-off from melting snow. These **prairie potholes** are the breeding grounds for nearly three quarters of all the ducks in North America. They are rich in plant and insect life. This invertebrate stew provides the breeding ducks with high protein meals.

Most ducks and geese nest in grassland cover near potholes. When the eggs hatch, the adults lead their young to the water. Small potholes dry out, so birds may live in several potholes before they are grown.

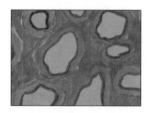

Long ago, a duck's-eye view of prairie potholes looked like this. In wet years, 6 million ponds could be found in prairie pothole country.

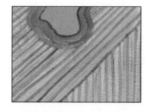

Today's duck's-eye view often looks like this. Potholes have been drained or filled in for agriculture or development.

Invertebrate Stew

Take one prairie pothole, warm to 60° F, and stir in:

1. 100,000 fairy shrimp
2. 5,000 water tigers
3. 100,000 mosquito larvae
4. 2,000 small snails
5. Add 100 bunches of duck potatoes, also called arrowhead.
6. Garnish with duckweed.

Serves a large party of ducks.

Match pictures with ingredients in recipe.

24

Migration Ups and Downs

A migration is a seasonal journey from one area to another. Many water birds nest in wetlands in the north. When the chicks are grown and freeze-up threatens, the birds fly south to the spend the winter where the weather is milder and food more plentiful. Along the way, the birds need food and rest. Over time, wetlands have been drained. In many places, fewer than half of our original wetlands remain. This spells TROUBLE for many migrating birds.

Game: Can your flock survive the journey to its northern breeding grounds and back?

You will need:
- A playing piece. Use a pebble or a coin, or trace one of the birds below, cut it out, color it, and tape it to a penny.
- Four objects (paper or pebbles) numbered 1, 2, 3, and 4. You could use a die and ignore 5 & 6.
- Pencil and paper to keep track of the number of birds left in your flock.

Canada Goose

Pintail Duck

Trumpeter Swan

Sandhill Crane

Directions:

1. Place your playing piece on START. Each piece is a flock of 100 birds.

2. Draw a number or roll the die. As you move your flock, follow instructions, keeping track of the number of birds left.

3. This circle with a pintail duck is a rest stop symbol. When you land here, rest safely.

4. Each flock must stop at the Summer Nesting Grounds. Figure out the number of breeding pairs in your flock by dividing by 2.

5. Cranes lay 2 eggs per pair; others lay 3. Multiply the number of eggs by the number of pairs and add them to your flock. (In nature birds lay more or fewer eggs.)

6. Complete the nesting ground loop, stopping at the Staging Grounds, where the birds set up a temporary home before flying South.

7. Return to the wintering ground, still keeping track of the number of birds.

8. As flocks arrive, food is used up. To find out how many birds survive in your flock, use this chart:
   - First flock counts all birds.
   - Second flock loses 4 birds.
   - Third flock loses 8 birds.
   - Each flock loses 4 more birds than the previous one.
   Each flock that returns with at least 100 birds is a winner.

Why do cranes have an especially hard time?

25

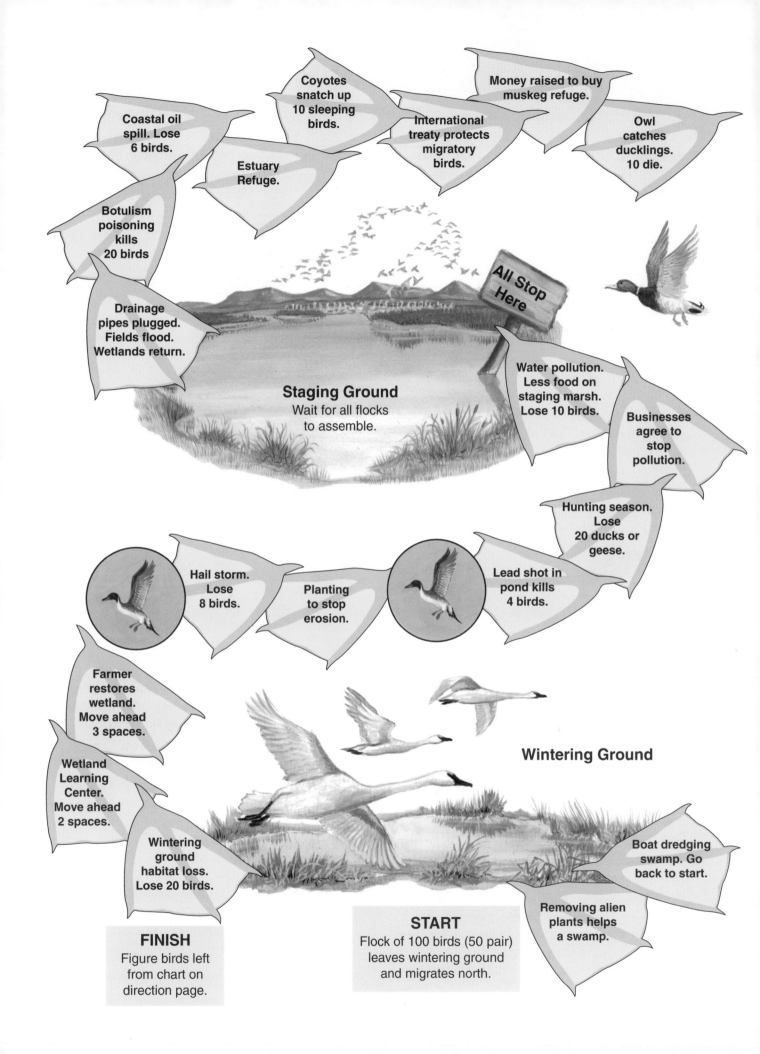

Sandhill cranes lay again. Replace lost eggs.

12 birds killed by other fledglings.

Cattle kept off marsh. More cover. Move ahead 2 spaces.

Nesting platform built for ducks and geese.

Hen houses provide nesting sites. All eggs hatch.

Dam causes flooding. Lose 16 eggs.

All Stop Here

Summer Nesting Ground
Count birds. Divide by 2. Cranes lay 2 eggs per pair. Other birds lay 3 eggs per pair. Add eggs to flock .

Skunks eat 12 eggs and 6 hens.

Late snow storm and cold weather cause 20 eggs to freeze.

Prairie pothole drained. Farm crops planted. Lose 12 birds.

Thick fog. 8 birds collide with fire tower and die.

Outbreak of avian cholera. Disease kills 12 birds.

Marsh restoration project. Soar ahead 2 spaces.

New law saves this bog.

Pose for bird watchers photo.

Countries around the world have agreed to set aside wetlands of "international" significance. Now this marsh will always be protected.

Hungry bald eagles. Lose 6 birds.

Cranes Only

Escape fox. Fly ahead 1 space.

Flock runs into power lines. Lose 10 birds.

City greenbelt protects marsh. Soar ahead 3 spaces.

Bulldozer filling in marsh for apartments and airport. 6 birds die.

Bad storm delays migration. Lose 16 birds.

South wind. Push ahead 2 spaces.

Peat Bogs — Long Term Storage

Peat bogs are found in northern areas around the world. The most common plant in a peat bog is a moss with spongy leaves called **sphagnum moss**. Bogs are poorly drained and very acid. This is a tough environment for bacteria and the other decomposers. They cannot break down all the plant material. Over time, dead plants pack down into dense mats of **peat**, which looks like dark soil. Peat is coal in the making. Both peat and coal can be burned as fuel.

Black Spruce

Larch

Fens are similar to peat bogs, but some water flows through them. Grasses, sedges and reeds grow in fens. If the water stops flowing through a fen it gradually becomes a bog.

Pete Moss says bogs are like history books. They tell the story of the past. People digging in a bog in Chile found tent poles tied together with twine that was 12,500 years old. They could even tell what stone-age people had for dinner–chunks of mastodon meat and potatoes.

One letter at a time . . .

. . . change a peat to a coal

P	E	A	T	used for fuel
_	_	_	_	animal skin
_	_	_	_	worn around waist
_	_	_	_	you can ring it
_	_	_	_	weevil in cotton
_	_	_	_	water can at 100° C
_	_	_	_	ring or spiral of rope
C	O	A	L	used for fuel

Sphagnum moss

. . . change a fen to a bog

F	E	N	wetland with slowly moving water
_	_	_	helps a fish swim
_	_	_	fruit
_	_	_	thick mist
B	O	G	wetland with acid soil and standing water

Answers on last page

Most plants cannot survive in a peat bog. Important nutrients are missing because the decomposers could not do their job. Two kinds of plants have found an unusual way to get missing nutrients. They have added insects to their dinner menu. The sundew and pitcher plant both earn the description "beautiful but deadly!"

A frog zaps a bug with its sticky flypaper tongue. It usually blinks when it swallows. Its eyeballs help force the food down to its stomach.

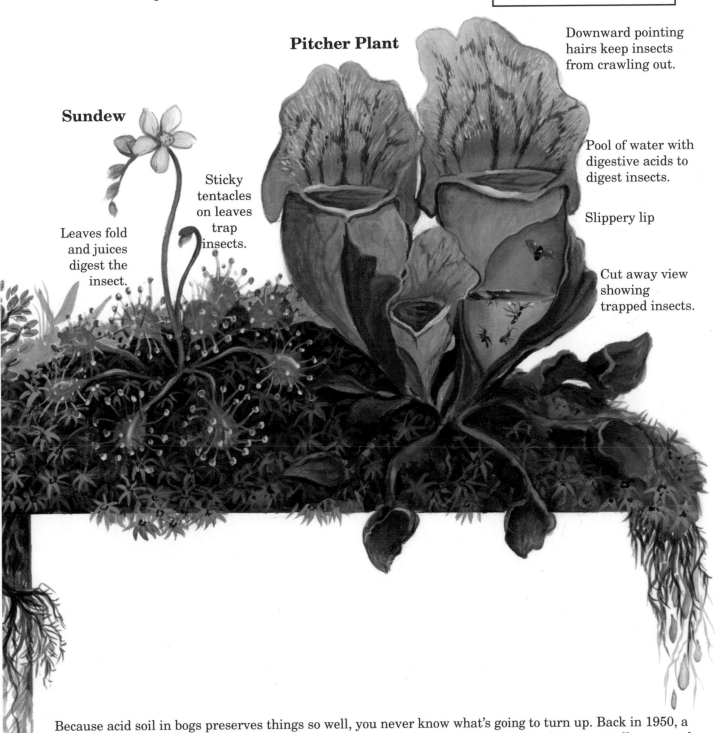

Pitcher Plant

Downward pointing hairs keep insects from crawling out.

Sundew

Sticky tentacles on leaves trap insects.

Leaves fold and juices digest the insect.

Pool of water with digestive acids to digest insects.

Slippery lip

Cut away view showing trapped insects.

Because acid soil in bogs preserves things so well, you never know what's going to turn up. Back in 1950, a farmer in Denmark found a 2,000-year-old body in a bog. It had become a mummy. It was so well preserved that the police could take his fingerprints. The mummy had a rope around his neck, but we don't know if he was a criminal or a victim. **Draw some artifacts for Pete Moss to find in the bog.**

Hiding in a Cypress Swamp

A cypress can live for 500 years, but not many trees are that old. Earlier this century, most cypress forests were cut. The wood is valuable timber because it does not rot. Today most old trees are protected, but even young trees look ancient with their knobbly knees sticking up from the water and their long beards of Spanish moss.

The dim light of the cypress swamp is a great place for playing hide-and-seek. Animals depend on camouflage to help them hide from predators. Predators rely on camouflage, too. The odds are better if the prey doesn't see them coming.

Here's a list of creatures lurking in the swamp: alligator, turtle, snake, dragonfly, tree frog, grasshopper, ants, snail, raccoon, bear, duck, stork, egret, and butterfly. How many can you find?

The little grass frog is good at hiding. When fully grown, it is only about half an inch long.

Cypress Knees

Scientists do not really know what cypress knees are for. Maybe they help anchor the trees in the wet soil. Maybe they send oxygen to the roots.

Saving the Shoreline

Some jobs require special skills. If you have those special skills, you are more likely to get the job. Les C. Beach is looking for a tree to protect the Florida coastline. Help him decide who gets the job.

HELP WANTED

Needed — a tree that can:

1. tolerate salt water;
2. anchor the shoreline and prevent erosion;
3. protect land from hurricanes;
4. provide perching and nesting sites;
5. add nutrients to the environment.

Apply to Les C. Beach ,
Florida Coast

Wood Stork

Egret

Live babies: The mangrove seed starts to grow while still attached to the parent tree. Some seeds stick in the mud where they fall and start to grow. Others float until their roots drag on the bottom.

I am a mighty oak. Choose me!

I am very strong and live for a long time.
My spreading branches provide perches
and nesting sites.
My acorns are food for many kinds of animals.
My leaves decay slowly.
My roots are wide spread and deep.
I am from a family with sea going experience.
My ancestors were made into sailing ships.

*Les C. Beach got out
his dictionary.
hal.o.phyte *n* a plant
that grows in salty soil.

I am a red mangrove. Choose me!

I am a halophyte. *
I protect the land behind me from hurricanes.
Birds roost and nest in my branches.
My leaves fall twice each year and rot quickly. Rotten leaves are good food!
My prop and drop roots take oxygen from the air and send it to underground roots.
My tangled roots anchor the shoreline and provide shelter. They trap food brought in by the tide.
If I get the job, my offspring will work for you, too, though some may take off for distant places.
We are great travelers when we are young, but if we settle down, we're here to stay.

Which tree deserves the job? _____

Answers on last page

How Lowly Muskrat Saved the Earth

Long before the first Europeans came to these shores, the Native Americans valued the plentiful animal life of the wetlands. They hunted ducks, geese, fish, muskrats and many other animals for food. They harvested wild rice and water lily tubers. They made baskets, mats, and shelters from rushes. They watched the rise and fall of the water with the seasons.

An Ojibwa story tells how lowly Muskrat helped Wenaboozhoo create a new Earth after the Great Flood. When the waters covered the land, Wenaboozhoo saved himself by climbing onto a floating log. There wasn't enough room on the log for everyone. Four-leggeds, Crawlers, and Winged Creatures took turns swimming and resting.

Wenaboozhoo decided to dive deep into the floodwater and bring back a handful of Earth. With the Creator's help, he would make a new place for the land creatures. He was gone so long that the animals thought he had drowned. At last, he came back to the surface, spluttering and gasping, but he brought back no earth. The water was too deep.

"Let me try!" said Loon.

Loon gave nearly all her strength, but the water was too deep. Wenaboozhoo revived her, holding her gently in his hand

Helldiver, a grebe, took his turn and then Otter. As Wenaboozhoo revived each animal, his heart grew heavier. Was there no hope for a new Earth?

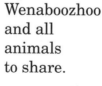

Finally, only Muskrat was left. The other animals sneered when he offered to try. How could lowly Muskrat succeed where they had failed? When Muskrat's limp body floated to the surface, it seemed that they had been right. Wenaboozhoo held the little animal tenderly, as he had the others, but muskrat's spirit had left him. Then Wenaboozhoo noticed a small ball of earth in the tiny clenched fist. Muskrat had done it! But he had given his life to bring them a new Earth.

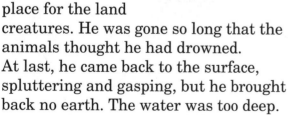

Wenaboozhoo placed the little ball of earth on the back of Turtle. The winds began to blow. Earth grew and grew until it became Turtle Island, a new Earth, a place for Wenaboozhoo and all animals to share.

Harvesting wild rice

World wide, rice is the most important wetland crop, but other foods grow in wetlands, too.

Use the code to discover what's on the menu at the Gourmet Wetlands Cafe.

1. | 19 | 8 | 5 | 12 | 12 | 6 | 9 | 19 | 8 |
| | | | | | | | | |

5. | 23 | 9 | 12 | 4 | | 18 | 9 | 3 | 5 |
| | | | | | | | | |

2. | 3 | 18 | 1 | 14 | 2 | 5 | 18 | 18 | 25 | relish
| | | | | | | | | |

6. | 23 | 1 | 20 | 5 | 18 | 3 | 18 | 5 | 19 | 19 | garnish
| | | | | | | | | | |

3. | 19 | 8 | 18 | 9 | 13 | 16 |
| | | | | | |

4. boiled | 3 | 1 | 20 | 20 | 1 | 9 | 12 | 19 |
| | | | | | | | |

People who like to eat frog legs introduced bull-frogs in new areas. With their big mouths and big appetites, bullfrogs out-eat the smaller frogs that belong there. Introduced animals and plants can often cause big problems. Purple loosestrife is plant enemy number one in many wetlands.

SECRET CODE:

1	2	3	4	5	6	7	8	9	10	11	12	13	14	15	16	17	18	19	20	21	22	23	24	25	26
A	B	C	D	E	F	G	H	I	J	K	L	M	N	O	P	Q	R	S	T	U	V	W	X	Y	Z

Answers on last page

Wetlands in Your Own Back Yard

Wetlands can be found in every state and province in North America. There's probably one near your home. Many are small. A fun group project is to visit the same wetland during different seasons and notice how the water level and plants change. It takes time to get to know a wetland.

Make sure you are well prepared before you set out on your wetland expedition. Wear tall rubber boots. You'll need a book to help you identify the plants and birds. A sketching pad and a camera are useful tools for recording what you see. Copy the sheet on page 38 so that you can record your observations. If the wetland is on private property, be sure to get the owner's permission to study it.

Your Own Wetland Record Sheet

Observer _____

Date _____

Time _____

Weather _____

Water depth:

    Point A_____

    Point B_____

    Point C_____

Soil (feel, color, smell)

_____

_____

_____

Map or Picture

Plants (submerged, floating, and emergent)

Animals and signs of animals

Changes from last time visited:_____

_____

_____

_____

Marsh Hawk

Wetland Puzzlers

When you complete these puzzles, you'll find the three keys that help decide if wet land is in fact a wetland. If you are having trouble guessing a word from the clue, the number in brackets provides the page where the word occurs.

Mink

1. water that is part salty, part fresh (18)
2. type of amphibian (2)
3. describes wetland soil (9)
4. a fossil fuel (4)

5. a wetland with trees and shrubs (16)
6. a tree with stilt and prop roots (33)
7. where a river meets the sea (18)
8. to break down or rot (9)
9. seasonal journey (25)

10. small prairie wetland (24)
11. reptile in the Everglades (20)
12. a dam builder (14)
13. soil that lacks oxygen (9)
14. areas that belong to the water and the land (2)
15. a dragonfly, for example (15)

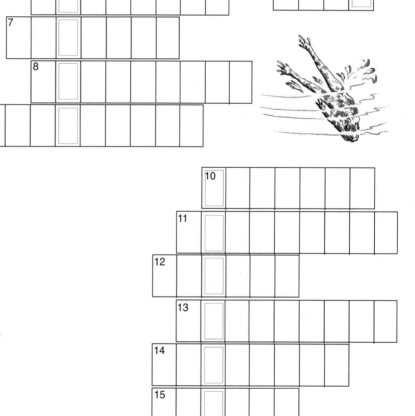

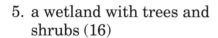

Answers

Avocet

p. 5 1 – water; 2 – soil; 3 – plants;   **p.7** 1 – C; 2 – A; 3 – B

p. 9 The pans with the gravel and sand will fill the fastest.
Under the right conditions, wetland soil is the best filter.
You may have to put water through once or twice to get this result.

p. 13 A–Canoe–recreation; B–Mosquito–link in food chain; C–Net–strains silt
and debris from water; D–Sponge–soaks up flood water; E–Shark–affect ocean;
F–Soap–cleaning; G–Bed–resting place for migrating birds; H–Camera–nature
watching; I–Shield–storm protection; J–Plate–food supply; K–Cradle–nursery for young creatures.

p. 14 5, 1, 3, 4, 6, 2   **p.15** A — 4; B — 1; C — 5; D — 2; E — 6; F — 3

p. 16 A - Swamp, B - Marsh; Pronunciation: **Muskeg**-*MUS keg* ; **Slough**-*SLOO* ; **Bayou**-BY you

p. 21 Babysits; makes pools; nest is a good place for plants to grow

p. 22

16	Water site	20	Mole nest site
1, 6	Moose birth	2	Whitetailed deer
2, 5, 7, 9	Moose food	4	Spiders
14	Skunk cabbage	17	Alder flycatcher
4	Honey bees	3	Woodcock food
2	Ruffed grouse	13	Frog food
11	Warblers	5, 10, 12, 18, 19 -	
8	Moles tunnel		Bear food
3, 15	Mole food	9	Green heron hiding

p. 19 Frogs don't live in salt water.

p. 39

S	W	A	M	P

M	A	N	G	R	O	V	E

E	S	T	U	A	R	Y

D	E	C	O	M	P	O	S	E

M	I	G	R	A	T	I	O	N

B	R	A	C	K	I	S	H

F	R	O	G

H	Y	D	R	I	C

C	O	A	L

P	O	T	H	O	L	E

A	L	L	I	G	A	T	O	R

B	E	A	V	E	R

A	N	A	E	R	O	B	I	C

W	E	T	L	A	N	D	S

I	N	S	E	C	T

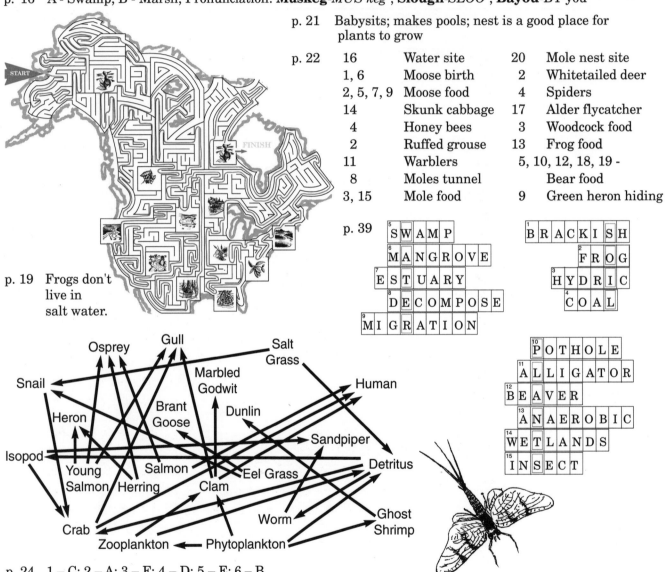

p. 24 1 – C; 2 – A; 3 – F; 4 – D; 5 – E; 6 – B

p. 28 FEN – FIN – FIG – FOG – BOG; PEAT – PELT – BELT – BELL – BOLL – BOIL – COIL – COAL

p. 32 The red mangrove gets the job

p. 35 1 – SHELLFISH; 2 – CRANBERRY; 3 – SHRIMP; 4 – CATTAILS; 5 – WILD RICE; 6 – WATERCRESS

Dog-Eared Publications thanks: Wildlife biologists, Don Progulske, Dick Taber and Jim Fisher, Delta Waterfowl, college instructor Sally DeRoo, and naturalists Sue Bridson and Nancy Dott for reviewing the book and Jon Netherton for allowing us to illustrate the frog on page 10 from his photograph in the book *Frogs*.